According to the dictionary , the word "*Fair*" means treating people equally without favouritism or discrimination, and it is also used to describe the complexion of the skin.

My Fair Uncle

.... is a story of a struggling young girl called Sussan. Sussan Okigbo was born in Benue state, Nigeria, to very poor parents, Mr and Mrs Okigbo. Her childhood days weren't so pleasant as expected, it was full of nightmares. Her mother was a disciplinarian who struggled night and day to help raise up a family of five children.

Even with the poverty at home, family relatives travelled from far and near to spend days at the Okigbo's. Why were they visiting?

A family who found it difficult to make ends meet regularly had male relatives pouring in for whatever reason.

The simple reason was Sussan. Being the only girl child in the extended family made her feel like a princess, and she was treated as one. No family member visited empty handed, each one had one sort of present , toys or another. It took years for Mrs Okigbo to know why.....

On one dark day, some male relative came visiting;

"My little princess, how are you today"? Uncle Tom called out with a pink Barby doll waving in the air..

"Susu come here"! he shouted a second time knowing full well that her parents were not at home. Her parents were Jehovah witnesses who shared door to door messages to people in the neighbourhood and they were on the normal routine of evangelizing when Tom visited.

Uncle Tom had travelled down from Jos, Plateau state in Nigeria to visit the Okigbo's.

He usually got a clue from a neighbour concerning the whereabouts of the Okigbo's.

These relatives were actually coming to molest little Sussan. But as fate would have it, she fled way from home at the age of 10 to the riverine area , Delta state in Nigeria.

An aunt, the complete opposite of her mother , was the one living in Delta State. Aunt Meg, an unbeliever, contrary to her Jehovah witness mother was an awful sight to behold every morning. Apart from being so vain, she hardly made sense whenever she talks.

Sussan travelled through the night to start a new life in Warri. Thank God for night buses, she exclaimed!

Although she had left home in the morning to avoid travelling in the night, her journey wasn't successful .

She boarded a taxi van that apparently had mechanical problems. None of the passengers noticed the problems until the car broke down somewhere along Oturkpo road in Benue state. The taxi driver couldn't make any refunds because journeys in Nigeria are paid for at the Car Parks.

So Sussan had to just stick with the driver till his car was fixed and in order. The car actually broke down twice (once at Oturkpo and a second time at ninth mile corner, in Enugu state) making the journey seem endless and tiresome.

Luckily she wasn't travelling alone. She travelled in the company of some students and their teachers, so it wasn't obvious that she was running away.

A 6-hour journey turned into an unending 15-hour one. At 8pm in the evening, she was already at Onitsha city in Nigeria. She wasn't bothered at all rather her only worries were her parents back home in Benue State and not in the direction where she was heading. She wasn't expected by her aunt and luckily at that time, the mobile phones weren't yet invented. Only the pay phone installed by the Nigerian Telecommunication services (NITEL) were in operation.

She actually wanted to call her aunt to make sure she was still in Delta state using the coins she was given by the driver to buy water because she was thirsty. This gesture was a kind of compensation for lost hours but she changed her mind suddenly and it was while making a turn she bumped into a stranger, a young man, who was also travelling that night. She had just a hand bag but the bag appeared heavy, she was exhausted. The stranger took her by the hand and helped her with her bag while murmuring some words to her

"Young girl, where are you going to? The next bus is about to depart, let's hurry" the voice said.

"I am travelling to Delta sir, is the bus going to Delta state"? Sussan asked

"Yes, I am travelling there too, we have to hurry".

That was how she was able to take a bus that night. She wasn't offered a seat but a stool to sit down because the spaces were all filled in.

Immediately tears ran down her cheeks and the man who gave her a helping hand asked her why the tears were on her cheeks.

"Why are you crying? Are you lost?

What is your name?" He continued without letting her answer one question before asking another.

"My name is Sussan sir, am travelling to my aunty and I don't know if she will be available, I am hungry and I haven't eaten since morning".

She continued, "As a matter of fact, I just want to sleep and I can't do that while sitting on this small stool. Please help me".

Immediately the man stood up and changed places with her. She fell asleep right on the bus without eating a thing.

She snored so hard that someone immediately tapped her on her back. To her greatest surprise, the bus had already arrived Benin City, and was parked at a gas station to buy diesel and allow the passengers who were travelling in the bus ease themselves and have refreshments.

Unknown to little Sussan, the owner of the gas station was an old friend of her aunt, Meg. His name was uncle Samuel. The family got to know Samuel because he intended marrying Meg, but because of her drunken ways, he married another woman and they recently heard that he has kids.

Sussan was travelling during the school vacation period and suddenly she remembered the school children she travelled with earlier on and their song again came to her lips. And just to keep her awake, she started whispering....

"Goodbye teacher

When do I get to see you, my dear teacher

I hope it won't be long"

Goodbye teacher, when do I get to see you, it may be far ,far away, bla bla"

It was at this time someone else in the night bus hit at the window just to make Sussan shut her mouth. Little did this fellow passenger know that he just did her a favour..

Sussan turned to her left to say sorry when she saw uncle Sam through the bus window. She ran out with her little bag and went to him.

He wasn't expecting to see her at all. He was shocked.

"Where are you going and what are you doing here at this time of the night"? He questioned..

"Uncle, hmmm, Sussan murmured,

I am travelling to Delta state to see aunt Meg. Frankly speaking, I don't have anywhere to go, I have been abused several times by my relatives who claimed to be my uncles.

My parents are so occupied with evangelism, they failed to see what's going on inside me.

I thought of Aunty Meg, I am going to see her and probably live with her for a while". She concluded.

"Do they know you left home? How could they allow you go to Meg?

That aunt of yours with her asininity?

Anyway, my wife just put to bed and we were searching for a maid to assist us, can you do that"? He asked further.

"Yes I can uncle, I will do anything just to go away from my parents and the molestation", she answered.

Ok, have you eaten? He asked further

"No, not at all, since morning, oh I mean

Since yesterday morning I left home to travel to Delta and the transport vehicle I took had broken down severally , now it is about 1am the next day". She answered.

"Ok , put your bag in my car. Get yourself some snacks from the shop to eat". He told her while pointing at the snack shop attached to the gas station.

"Thank you sir", she replied and then she hungrily grabbed some fried chicken and meat pie and some coca cola drinks.

The station closes at 5am each morning , so after eating, Sussan slept at back seat of uncle Samuel's car till he signed off for the day.

After work, Samuel brought Sussan to his wife, Perpetual, at home.

Perpetual isn't the down- to- earth type. She was a very sarcastic woman, with little or no respect for her husband. Samuel on the other hand was humble, God fearing and a truthful man. So it hurt him that he couldn't marry Meg, even though she was the love of his life. Perpy was his second best and because of timing, he settled for her.

Samuel's close pals knew about this story of he and Meg, and because of jealousy of his business, they went behind his back to tell Perpy.

So anything to do with the past and Meg, should be completely forgotten and this morning again, he reminisced, not only by bringing the little Sussan, he also talked about the good old days with her aunt Meg and Perpy wasn't happy. Her mood suddenly changed.

He introduced Sussan as Meg 's niece.

"Darling, this is Sussan, you remember Meg, my ex fiancé? This little girl is the daughter of Meg's sister"..

His wife Perpetual 's only reply was

"And then"?

"Darling, he called out again to his wife, what's wrong?

I told you it would be difficult for me to go at this moment to the village to get a house help, this is God's answer to our prayers, all we need do is enrol her in the nearby school so I can concentrate on my business.

You remember this is peak season? Travellers are everywhere and this is the time we make money selling gas at the station". He continued.

But before he could finish, his wife hissed passed him and went into their bedroom.

"Tell me you still love her, tell me you ingrate"....

Perpy ranted.

Meanwhile, Sussan was admiring their beautiful house , so she didn't notice the argument between the two.

He apologized to Sussan and told her to take her bag into the guest room while he had a chat with his madam.

On getting to the bedroom, his wife of 3 years suddenly changed.

"What is wrong again"? He asked

"Do you want to tell me I don't know the truth"? she asked.

"What truth? What are you talking about for God

sakes"?

"That Meg sent Sussan here to destroy our

marriage"….she replied

"You think I don't know too", she continued…

"That I was an alternative"? " You always wished

for Meg and since you couldn't have her, you

settled for me , bringing her niece here will

reignite whatever you felt for her, don't you think

so"?

"Oh common darling, not now he replied and

continued……

It's morning, I would expect you now to get acquainted with the fact that you are my one and only. Meg is my past. Sussan is here to help. This is our future now."

"Ok hon...if you say so, I will bring her to the guest room and then make sure she is registered at school immediately."

What seemed to be a happy home gradually started falling by day, with Sussan's arrival.

Sussan was gradually turned into a slave and it was from one lie to the other.

The problems started actually from Sussan's school. The school's principal was a friend to Perpy.

Although Sussan was very intelligent, she moved with some group of girls who were suspected to be thieves at school. One of the girls called Mandy was the leader of the girl's gang.

Whenever an item or money went missing, it was never found gain. She and her gang members had a special manner of hiding stolen things, and because of their regular routine of stealing, the entire school students were ransacked daily.

Each time Mandy or one of the gang members stole, the money was buried under the ground. A special knife was used to dig a hole in the soil or a nearby tree where the money is placed. It was always effortless searching or ransacking student school bags to find money that has been buried away somewhere.

Although Sussan moved with this gang members, she wasn't a thief.

Perpy got to hear of this news through the school principal. Even though Sussan didn't steal, her friendship with the gang made her an accomplice.

Instead of asking Sussan about the news and the gang, Perpy threw every belonging of Sussan out of the house before Samuel came back from a business trip.

Sussan had already made friends with some fellow Jehovah witnesses in the area where she stayed . She conveniently moved her belongings to the local assembly, it was then her family back in Benue state were contacted.

Her parents came running to Benin City where she was. There and then her father and mother got to know why she fled away from home. Although Samuel had called to tell them that they need not worry because she was with him, because of poverty, they couldn't make it a point of duty to run after their daughter.

The public transport fares where too high, especially with the problems of fuel shortage or scarcity at those times and their inability to pay her school fees made things worse.

Sussan had narrated how she lost her innocence to some relatives who visited back then in Benue state, and how her parents where so involved in the work of evangelism.

"I am not saying evangelism is not good, but daddy, you left me at the mercy of your brothers and after raping me, they made sure that they bathed me and put me to sleep with some medication". She said while sobbing...

"I was always given tea to drink, thereafter, I fell asleep. These people stay with us for two weeks monitoring me if I will speak about what they did to me". She continued burying her head in between her hands.

I had no other option but to run and in the process of running, I met uncle Samuel.

Today, I am back on the streets. Where do I go from here"? Sussan asked in tears.

"You are coming back with us today, we are sorry about this". Mr and Mrs Okigbo said at the same time.

"To be raped again"? Sussan asked..

"I can never go back home, I am sorry dear parents, I would rather continue my journey now to Delta state to meet aunty Meg.

I would go back home if you assure me you will keep things under control.

Come to think of it, the fear the memories would bring while I go back home will be too much for me to bear.

Consider it that you have lost a daughter. I am not trying to be disobedient to the principles you taught me, but memories of the pain I suffered at home will never let me rest." She said in a very touching speech.

The head of the assembly persuaded her to go with her parents, but she refused.

She was left to travel to Delta state and aunty Meg was informed about her coming.

Aunty Meg was the owner of a local bar and eatery in a city called Warri, in Delta state, Nigeria. She had girls Sussan's age working in her bar.

As a niece, Sussan was meant to go to school and not be a sale's girl but she was expected to join in the affairs of running the eatery. After school, without doing her homework, Sussan joins in serving food and drinks to customers.

Aunty Meg already knew about Sussan's molestation back in Benue state. She tried the best she could to avoid the fact that drunken customers do not end up making passes at her. Although Meg asininity almost ruined her life, some things she did or said still made sense.

Sussan wasn't a virgin anymore. She lost it quite early in life. And then all of a sudden, she lost her moral senses while serving at the bar.

Warri was a kind of congested town with a lot of people riding on motor bikes. It had a refinery and any man working then at the refinery was considered a rich man and they were good catches for young girls.

Young girls (between age 12-18) would pretend to leave home for school wearing school uniforms but on the way to school or after school depending on the programs on their hidden agenda, they changed from their school uniforms into *"muftis"* , a slang commonly used then by these under- aged girls.

A lot of the bar customers where rich refinery workers who came accompanied by girls Sussan's age. These men always showered money on these young girls, and bought them a lot of gifts. They were pampered by old men who were old enough to be their fathers. And most of it all, they were paid for sex. The law and the society didn't care about the girl child or the abuse.

Sussan became popular among these girls because her aunt was the owner of the bar where they all got together .

One particular customer found Sussan attractive. This customer (Mr Paul Ataka) was a confidant of Sussan's aunt. Aunt Meg had told him about the reason why Sussan came running to Warri.

Instead of helping matters, he joined to make it worse. Every now and then, he had presents for Sussan.

One day the following conversation ensued between them;

"Sussan come here right away", he said, calling her without respect. He was seen by the girls in the bar as a second boss.

According to available information, he was the guy who donated money to set up the bar. So his word was final with respect to matters regarding the bar and its activities.

"Yes sir", she replied, while attending to another male customer who was trying to play pranks with Sussan. Paul was jealous, but why?

He wanted to have sex with Sussan, and also make her his third wife. He had already spoken to Meg about the issue and also warned sternly that he didn't want her messing up with any customer otherwise the bar would be closed down.

Not only was the bar his major contribution, the apartment where Aunt Meg lived in was also his, so he was the money lender who made his borrowers his servants. They should be at his beck and call. Everything she had was also his.

Paul and Meg were actually lovers at first, and then he decided since he couldn't marry her, to open a bar for her where she could make ends meet. From her monthly savings, she acquired a car.

All the while, Meg never told anyone about the source of her wealth. She would always travel down to Benue state then to visit Sussan's family to tell lies about how God has blessed her with a lot of money and the new car. But now, the story changed.

Sussan also noticed how Paul would shout at Meg anytime she is also fooling around with a customer.

One day Sussan was prompted to ask her who Paul was...

"What are you doing with the idiot there"? Paul asked Sussan.

"Nothing sir, I was only trying to serve him his drink and he started making fun of my hair". She replied.

"Are you here to make fun"?

"Come here, you little girl", he beckoned to her while leading her to an inner room in the apartment .

The bar was built in a way that it was somehow connected with the apartment, it was constructed with a remaining piece of land in front of the small apartment. After work, Aunt Meg and Sussan didn't have to take transport home, their apartment was just behind the bar.

"Didn't your aunty tell you"? He asked

"Tell me what sir"? She replied.

"That I am going to marry you and make you my third wife"? He asked further

It was then Aunty Meg walked in and joined the conversation.

Is it not too early? She asked.

"Early for what? While I sit here and watch my future wife mess around with some small boys here in Warri? I won't allow that. The earlier she puts the idea in her skull and dull brain, the better for all of us.

Meg, he continued...you know what you stand to lose if you do not co-operate"?

Please tell her now before it is too late, he said ,while walking away from both of them..

"Aunty Meg, are you going to just marry me off like that without prior information and my parent's consent"? Sussan asked.

I was going to tell you but out of fear, I just couldn't, knowing what you have already suffered sexually; she replied.

Luckily on that day, Meg was not drunk. On a drunken day, she would insult Sussan reminding her of how she was bought over by a piece of Barby doll, and now Paul was offering something better than a doll.

She didn't humiliate Sussan on this day but they both sat down to think of a plan on how to eliminate Paul, he was a threat to both of them.

"You know Paul has two wives already", Meg said.

"Yes aunty", Sussan replied.

"I refused to marry him because he wanted me to be a third wife, I am satisfied with all the financial support I am getting from him, I did not want any commitments, and not with you and him either.

We are going to work on a plan, yes, a vicious one and I don't care"... she continued.

"What do you want us to do"? Sussan asked.

"It is simple...we 'll poison his meal with some rat poison called *"Otapiapia"*.

"Otapiapia" was in vogue then. It was a poison used in killing rats and roaches at home. Heartless

people used it in poisoning loved ones, it was a way of getting rid of people by killing them slowly.

After having dinner here, we would persuade him to go home immediately and die with his wives"....she said suggestively.

"No, no, nooooo, I won't do this with you", Sussan replied.

Before she could finish saying no, a hot slap descended on her face.

Aunty Meg slapped the hell out of Sussan.

"You foolish girl. You think I wasn't told about your gang at school when you stayed with Samuel?

Samuel came to Warri every weekend to buy tanks of petrol, there wasn't any time he didn't pass by here to say hi to me. I knew you were living there.

So if you could join a girl's gang at school, why won't you play along with me in this game of eliminating Paul?

I was only going to be his victim, but now that you are here, you would do as I say otherwise, you would have yourself to blame for all this" , she said, while slamming the door at Sussan 's face.

It was then that it dawned on Sussan that she needed to pray, pray again because she hadn't prayed for a long time.

All the while she was with Meg, she couldn't join the assembly anymore because the bar was opened almost every day, including Sundays, and Meg wasn't a believer as such.

She took her bible and started praying.

She prayed to God to help and forgive her.

The next day, the news that Warri was going to join the global village through the dawn of the use of the Global systems for mobile communication (GSM) filled the air.

Meg and Sussan were among the ladies to own a mobile phone in Warri. Paul made that possible.

Paul gave the phone set to Sussan so she is always aware of his coming to the bar and also to pre-inform her about what he intended eating. He started having sex with her already. At her age, she knew everything there was to know about men. She looked older than girls of her age because of molestation.

She was also obliged to take the phone to school. Sussan attended a mixed school (a school attended by both boys and girls) where Paul's nephew was also a student. Whenever Sussan talked with any boy at school, she was reported to Paul, it was from one bullying to another.

One day, on the 1st of May (workers day) precisely, she had a call from Paul that they were going to visit cinema together and afterwards, he would take her to the river to swim.

"Hallo, hallo my dear, did you sleep well"? He asked.

"Yes sir", she replied...

"Stop this "sir" thing, ok, from now on your reply should be *"Nkem"*, meaning my own in Igbo Language,

Did you understand?" shouting at the top of his voice while talking to her on the phone.

She didn't decline, she said "ok".

It was that day, she needed to flee .

Next to the bar was a hotel, (Prime star hotel, a very big one for that matter. Only the high and the mighty in the society lodges there. It was a long weekend and with May day, people came from different parts of the country into that hotel to celebrate workers day. And among these people was a chief Magistrate and his two sons aged 25 and 19 years respectively.

Their father was there in Warri to start a criminal proceeding. Although the magistrate had a kind of strict life, he was a drunk. He avoided drinking or eating in the hotel where ever he lodges, instead he prefers going to local bars where no one would notice or recognise him.

It was a day to liberate Sussan from her bondage. They all visited Aunty Meg's bar and there they met Sussan.

Sussan's phone was tied to her apron. She always wore a uniform to serve at the bar and in front of her uniform was an apron where she dumps her tips from customers.

"Good afternoon all" ..the well-mannered magistrate Owoh greeted.

"Good afternoon, sir" and what may I offer you all.

(He came into the bar accompanied by his two sons)

Yes, young lady. It would be a bottle of Star Lager beer for me and for these two , a bottle of Fanta and Coca cola each.

"Do you people have fried meat? You may serve some along with the drinks". He continued, while clearing his throat.

"Ok sir" ..Sussan replied.

It was while serving the dinks and meat that her phone rang again….

It rang so loud that the magistrate panicked. He was an old man of about 70years old, about to go on pension.

"What was that young lady? Are you planning a coup"? The magistrate asked.

Everyone laughed, including his son, Tema, who was already eyeing Sussan.

"No daddy", Tema replied, it is the GSM , it is the fashion now.

I wonder how she got one of those. She is too young for that. At that time, the mobile phones were only for parents and not meant for children.

Tema put in a word again…"you see daddy, I have been asking you to buy me a mobile phone, you refused claiming that it was only for big people, see now, an ordinary sales girl has one".

It was then the magistrate asked her

"My daughter, how did you come about having a mobile phone"?

Coincidentally, the magistrate was also a Jehovah's witness.

The question made Sussan to take a seat and on the table where she sat was a Jehovah's witness pamphlet .

She put her head on the pamphlet and tears filled the table.

"We didn't come here to make you cry, please my child, raise up your head.

Is your mother the owner of this place? Go and call her, I have questions for her". He said.

"No, no, no, no, no sir, please, please, you people just have your drinks and go away...please", She insisted.

It was then Tema intruded,

 "Daddy stop, let me handle this".

Tema gave Sussan their hotel room number and told her she was welcomed to talk, anytime she closed from the bar, she could come and pay them a visit.

Sussan did pay them a visit. It was then she told them about the story of her life and how badly she would love to go away.

After his criminal proceedings at the local court, the chief magistrate and his two sons went back to Benin City with Sussan. She fled without saying a word to Meg.

Meg should take care of the mess she put herself into, she cannot use Sussan to clean up her mess.

Before Sussan left Meg, she called her parents informing them of the development.

It was in Benin City, Nigeria, that she met my fair uncle.

My fair uncle, Mr Agbaje, is a man everyone in the family looked up to with respect.

He was the one that would speak for the entire extended family, in fact, he was the family's spokesman. He was academically inclined and he always insisted on children being properly educated and trained to go to school and become useful in life.

Although, Mr Agbaje was fair in complexion , he always used the word "fair" during his speech making.

During festive periods, whenever the whole extended family is gathered, he makes speeches and always ended each speech with the words

"I am just being fair with all of you". That is why we all called him "fair uncle".

And not only that, he was also the head of the human resources (*HR*) department at his place of work. So everyone thought that the word "fair" actually came from there. And we were right.

Uncle Agbaje only had the word "*Fair*" for intending applicants who weren't successful after a job interview like this one below

"Mr Jones, we are very sorry to say that you failed the interview for this job but it would be fair for us to say that you should re-apply, who knows, you might just be taken the next time.......bla bla bla".

And while in Benin City, Sussan became the house mother in the magistrate's household and she took care of his home well. The magistrate's wife of 40years left him because he wasn't happy their only daughter Sandra married a foreigner from Cameroon.

Sandra studied law at the university of Benin, Nigeria, and it was at the law school she met Klint, a Cameroonian .

Mr Owoh wanted her daughter to follow in his footsteps badly, but she eloped with the Cameroonian, so did his wife. Every time he had an opportunity to say the story, he always said it with passion and he was still hoping that one day, his wife and daughter would come back.

This was the reason he drank himself to stupor and whenever he went drinking, he was accompanied by his two sons who brought him back home safely.

Sussan had recently taken the West African Senior Certificate Examination. She credited all the courses except the English Language course. She couldn't gain admission into the university even though she had also passed the University Matriculation Exams.

Mr Owoh wasn't prepared to spend another money to enrol for an examination for Sussan, instead, she had to apply first for a job as a part time officer at the University's Human Resources Department just to get some money to re-write the entrance exams into the university.

And guess who she met on the day of the interview? She met "My fair uncle".

Before now, Sussan was introduced to me as a friend to another friend of ours, so we became friends automatically. She was new in town. We had to regularly help her get acquainted with the life in Benin City. Although she had been in Benin

City before, she lived then at a remote area far from the city centre where we were staying.

I was also trying then to gain admission into the Lagos State University. So I was regularly out of town. We only met when I was back home in Benin City.

It was on one of such visits that she told me she encountered problems during her exams and the magistrate is not willing to re-enrol her for another exam.

"So what do you intend doing now"? I asked her pitifully.

"I will try to get a job first at the university and thereafter re-enrol to write the exams again". She replied.

The next week she went for an advertised job vacancy, and it was our fair uncle who interviewed her and this dialogue ensued between them;

"You see young lady, I am very sorry that you didn't meet the criteria for the selection of an officer for this job". He said after the interview.

"How do you mean sir? But your office required 5 credit passes in all the courses but I had 7"? She defended herself further.

"Oh no, that is correct but you see, you failed in English", he replied.

"But it is very surprising that it is the same English language that you are speaking very well.

It would only be fair for me now to ask you to re-apply or give something in return . Maybe then I may perhaps reconsider you"...he continued with a smile.

Anyway wait in my office while I ask the other applicants to go home for the day.

It was there in the office that my fair uncle made love to Sussan.

This same man who preaches against bribery and corruption, and dishonesty at workplaces. At family meetings, he portrays an undaunted attitude and everyone looks up to him. No one ever suspected that he could be so foul in his

activities until he accidentally visited my parents

one day while Sussan was also visiting.

Sussan and I were in our living room watching TV

when he visited.

Sussan already made mention of a man who gave

her a job in return for sex but I never in my life

thought it was my fair uncle.

www.ingramcontent.com/pod-product-compliance
Lightning Source LLC
Chambersburg PA
CBHW071125280526
45787CB00003B/1172